HOW ONE
WEEKEND

CAN GIVE YOU
EVERYTHING

YOU EVER
WANTED

GRAHAM ALBANS

British Library Cataloguing in Publication Data
A record for this book is available from the British Library

ISBN: 978-1-837280-29-2

Designed and typeset by Pete Barnsley (CreativeHoot.com)

Printed in Denmark

10Publishing, a division of 10ofthose.com
Unit C, Tomlinson Road, Leyland, PR25 2DY, England

Email: info@10ofthose.com
Website: www.10ofthose.com

1 3 5 7 10 8 6 4 2

CONTENTS

'WHAT'S NEXT?'

It's the question I'd ask myself every morning.

For over a decade of my life, I climbed the career ladder with 'what's next?'. I got into being a radio producer through my university's student station, but the goal was always to work up. Through constantly asking 'what's next?', I found myself at BBC Radio 2 and eventually became the lead producer of the Breakfast Show, the most listened to radio show in Europe.

If you'd told teenage me – sat in a mate's lounge, filling in job applications, and watching Glastonbury on the telly – that I'd be having a cuppa with McCartney and sharing sandwiches with Sheeran, I think teenage me would have fallen over. All achieved from asking 'what's next?'.

But whatever level was reached, there was always another to reach for.

Maybe you can relate.

The question doesn't just get asked about our professional goals. We ask it about the stuff we own, as we keep levelling up our possessions and property to get a sense of significance. We ask it about our finances, as we look to clear debt or increase our bank balances to get a sense of security. We ask it as we build a family, parenting as best we can for a sense of meaning and happiness. We ask it about our bodies, as we set personal targets to feel better about ourselves. We ask it about our life experiences, as we optimistically look forward to the next holiday or milestone. Maybe we've even asked it about the person we're in a relationship with, as we search for 'the one'.

Nothing seems to be able to fully hold the weight of expectation we place on it. Even when things are going well in our lives, we can lack a deep sense of satisfaction and contentment. So often we're left wanting more.

As I'm sat writing the book you're holding in your hands, my phone pings. It's that same mate I applied for jobs with while watching

Glastonbury on TV. But this time he's actually there. His talent and determination led him to a job working with a global pop superstar. 'I'm losing my drive a little,' he messages. 'Weirdly, headlining Glastonbury doesn't feel like *enough* …'

'What's next?' I reply.

When do we get to stop asking that question? What are we looking for, with all our goals, relationships and life experiences? What is it that we all really want?

I believe we're all looking for the same fundamental things. We all want to live a contented life, where we feel satisfied. We're searching for love, happiness, freedom, peace. We want meaning, significance. We need hope. If you'll stick with me I'd love to give you at least a flavour of how just one weekend can give you everything you ever wanted.

But first we need to pin down which weekend we're talking about …

WHAT'S
THE STORY?

What are the ingredients of your ideal weekend? Maybe friends, family, food, fun, films, football … Personally I love getting out on a Saturday morning, watching my son's team, then cooking brunch with my daughter. I love a weekend.

But I've never had a weekend so good it's still talked about in nearly every nation on the planet two millennia later and has changed the lives of an estimated 2.4 billion people alive today, let alone down the centuries.

My brunches are good, but they're not *that* good!

The first Easter weekend was so good, they literally rebranded the opening day 'Good Friday'! Although, when you know the detail of what happened, there's not a lot that was obviously 'good' about it.

Around the age of 33, Jesus was arrested during the night, accused of stirring up trouble by claiming to be the Son of God, equal to God himself. In that particular time and place, this wasn't a claim that would get you a few funny looks and a social media shaming. It was the kind of claim that got you brutally tortured, then hammered to a wooden cross like a piece of butchered meat.

One Friday in spring on a hill outside first-century Jerusalem, that's what happened. Jesus – the one who had spent his life caring for the vulnerable, healing the sick, standing with the oppressed and welcoming the outcast – was battered, beaten, bruised and brutalised, then literally hung out to dry on a rough wooden stake in the ground. And all because he claimed to be God in the flesh.

Evening probably faded into a sleepless night for his first followers, and I can't imagine that Saturday to have been much fun. Devastation, disappointment, depression and distress would have ruled the day. They thought Jesus would be a hero for their people. But instead they'd seen his torn, dead body wrapped in bandages and placed in a borrowed grave.

On Sunday morning, some of the women in their group went to visit the tomb. But where there had once been a huge boulder over the entrance and armed Roman guards to keep away grave-robbers, the women found Jesus' body gone. Not stolen, or revived, or moved, but *gone*. Jesus wasn't there.

Over the coming hours and days, Jesus turned up in various places to various people. And not as a vision, but physically, in front of groups of eyewitnesses where he'd eat with them and walk with them and let them touch his wounds, because they couldn't quite believe what they were seeing (which, to be fair, is understandable!). Jesus wasn't dead anymore.

Little side note – if all that sounds a bit unbelievable, a bit far-fetched, trust me I totally get it. That's what led me to look into it for myself and find out whether there was a shred of historical, medical or archeological evidence to back up the claims of these events. Was it just a story, or did it really happen in history? The answer to that question is vital. I'd invite you to look into it further for yourself. One of the best short summaries of the overwhelming amount of evidence available is called *The Case For Easter*, and a copy can be yours by scanning the QR code at the back of this book.

Maybe you're familiar with that Easter story, or maybe it's the first time you've heard it. But either way, what on earth has that weekend got to do with me and you living a life of contentment, full of love, peace, freedom and everything else?

Let's find out.

LOVE

Victoria walked into a sun-soaked school classroom in early spring. She glided across to her desk in what seemed like hazy slow motion, and picked up the single red rose that had been left on it.

It was February 14th, and our teacher had come up with a plan that I'm sure must have seemed sweet at the time …

Every boy in the class would place their rose on the desk of the girl they liked. If the girl could guess who'd left them a floral favour, they would be paired up for the school Valentine's Disco. Beautiful or brutal? You decide.

My palms were clammy, planted facedown firmly in front of me. My rose was Victoria's rose. My nine-year-old heart was all for her heart.

She picked up the flower by the stem and gently spun it around a couple of times between her fingertips.

This was it. *Say Graham, please say Graham.*

The sun streamed through the window behind her, perfectly backlighting her face as her mouth finally opened to break the silence and whisper the name …

'Adam.'

Ouch.

That was the first time I experienced the crushing reality that pinning my hopes of happiness on a person could come up short. And it wasn't the last.

We look for love from all kinds of people: our boyfriends and girlfriends, our mates, our families, our spouses. We all want to be loved. We all want to be fully seen and fully known. We want to be fully accepted, even with our flaws and failings.

But to know we're 100% accepted, we need to be 100% honest. And there are things in my life that I can't be fully honest about. At least not with everyone. If you could fully see me – like really, properly know me and my thoughts

– there are things you would find incredibly *un*lovely about me.

Can you relate? We all have things we'd rather keep hidden. Why? Because our fear is that if a person really knew the full extent of those hidden things, they'd reject us. They wouldn't want much to do with us. They would find out things that would put them off ever loving us.

We can hide those things from each other. But we can't hide those things from God.

He fully sees you. He knows you inside out. He sees your every thought. He knows your deepest desires. He knows your history, your past, your secrets. The dark rooms of your heart we shut everyone out of – he knows what's behind those doors.

And yet, he still loves you. Loads.

A well-known line in the Bible says: 'For God so *loved* the world that he gave his one and only Son [Jesus], that whoever believes in him shall not die but have eternal life.'[1]

And then we get this line from Jesus: 'There is no greater love than to lay down one's life for one's friends.'[2] Jesus isn't just talking

---

1   John 3:16, NIV

2   John 15:13

hypothetically. It's the Thursday evening before 'Good' Friday and he knows he's just an hour or two away from being arrested. He knows he will be tortured and killed. He knows he will die on the cross the next day, not only to save his friends but also his enemies. And he's willingly letting it happen.

Why?

All those wrong things we keep hidden. All the things we can't be 100% honest about. Jesus' death on the cross was exactly *because of* all those things. He was taking on himself the punishment for our sin. We may not use the word 'sin' much these days, but the Bible uses it to describe the things we keep locked away in the dark rooms of our hearts.

One of the big themes of Jesus' teaching was the seriousness of sin (more serious than we tend to take it), and that it ultimately deserves the most serious of consequences – eternal death.

God knows every hateful thought, he hears every unloving word, he sees every selfish action. He sees it all and yet, in Jesus, he offers to absorb the cost of our sin instead of making us pay the price. Jesus dies in our place. That's love! Our hidden things mean he should reject us but instead he offers acceptance. He should condemn us but instead offers friendship.

He doesn't just tolerate you, or put up with you. He doesn't just ignore those things or turn a blind eye to them. He fully sees, and fully knows, and yet fully loves.

And when we accept his love we find it to be permanent. It'll never disappear, disappoint or dissatisfy.

That's a love we all want to find.

FREEDOM

'*Weight* is the word everyone uses.'

I'm in the pub with my friend Karen. She works with people struggling with debt and is telling me about her job helping them get debt-free.

'They say it feels like such a burden.'

Debt feels like carrying around a backpack, and each new bill is like another brick added to the load. Carrying it all around with you every waking moment takes its toll, affecting the way you view yourself, other people, all of life.

Whether or not you have financial troubles, imagine for a moment that you too are carrying around a backpack. Imagine that through your whole life you've been gaining bricks. But they're less to do with money, and more to do with morals. Every time you've not told the whole truth – another brick. Every time anger has got the better of you – another brick. Every time you've hurt someone or let them down – another brick. Every time you've thought something you'd rather keep hidden – another brick.

Maybe you already sense a real weight of guilt that's attached to so many of those things. New bricks. Every day. Your whole life. It can change how you view yourself, other people, all of life. The burden takes its toll.

'*Trapped* is the other word that gets used a lot.'

Karen goes on to tell me that a person dealing with debt can often feel there's no way out. No matter how hard they try to work it off, no matter what repayment plan they come up with, no matter who they know or how many application forms they complete, it feels like nothing will change.

Burdened … Trapped … It seems fitting then that sometimes the Bible uses the word 'debt' instead of the word 'sin'. It helps us see that all the wrong things we've ever done, said and thought put us in the relational red of our moral bank account with God.

Most of us think that we can come up with a sin repayment plan. If we can just work off the bad stuff by doing some good stuff, then God will be okay with us. If I can just get to the end of my life with the scales tipped in favour of my goodness, then that will outweigh any wrong I've done.

But the uncomfortable truth of the Bible is that 'the wages of sin is death'.[3] In other words, there is no repayment plan that's going to go well for us.

So if we can't work it off, or pay it back, or apply for some kind of moral loan, how can we get to be debt-free? How can we escape the trapping burden of sin and guilt we've been carrying our whole lives (even if we weren't fully aware of it)?

We need the person we're in 'sin-debt' to – God himself – to pay it off for us.

Jesus hung on the cross for about six hours. God's judgement was falling on sin and that judgement was death. Jesus would have known the end was coming. Exhausted, dehydrated, and in the most excruciating pain imaginable,

---

3   Romans 6:23

there's something he needed us to hear. So important, it was worth him pushing himself up on the nails that pierced his ankles and wrists in order to take a breath, scraping the flesh of his flogged back against the rough wood of the cross. With that breath came his final words …

'It is finished!'[4]

Done. Paid.

Jesus was paying the debt of sin. And he paid in full.

That's why Easter gives us true freedom, because it's on the cross that Jesus pays the bill. He takes the debt on himself. His death is the repayment plan. On the cross Jesus takes that awful backpack off your shoulders, and plunges it all the way into the depths of where it deserves to go. Gone. Finished.

No more carrying around the heavy burden of the guilt of past mistakes. The debt has been paid.

One of the people Karen told me about was Michelle[5] who had been in debt for years. But Karen was able to deliver some really good

---

4   John 19:30

5   Name has been changed

news one morning. The official letter had come through: her debts could be wiped for her.

'Michelle cried when we told her,' Karen recalls.

'You mean, I don't have to pay *anything*?'

'No,' Karen had replied. 'Nothing. You just need to say "Yes".'

Michelle – through big, sobby tears – thanked Karen. This would change how she views herself, how she views other people, how she views everything. It would give her a new lease of life to live differently, in a way that reflected her new-found freedom.

Easter is God's way of paying off our sin-debt on our behalf, and now there's nothing to pay. We can thank him for writing off the debt. This can change how we view ourselves, others, everything. It can give us a new lease of life to live differently, in a way that reflects our new-found freedom.

All Michelle had to say was 'Yes, please' and freedom would be hers.

All you have to pray is 'Yes, please' and freedom can be yours.

SIGNIFICANCE

'Nice to meet you, Graham. What do you do?'

'Well, I used to be a national radio producer but now I'm a local church leader.'

'Oh.' Awkward silence as the person I'm talking to tries to work out a response to this.

I fill the gap. 'And what do you do?'

It's likely you've been asked the same thing many times: 'What do you *do*?' It's as though everything they need to know about you is wrapped up in whatever comes out of your mouth next.

So what do you tell them?

If you work, you tell them what you do. If you're retired, you tell them what you used to do. If you're between jobs, you tell them what you'd like to do. If you're a full-time parent, you tell them about your kids. If you're not sure where you fit, you make something up.

In the conversation that follows, you'll either have a sense of esteem or embarrassment. Why? Because what you do gives you a sense of value. The way you answer the question can feel like a judgement on what you're worth. Your significance is tied to your role in life, and how well it is going.

The problem is, what we do can often seem pretty insignificant compared to other people. We post our lives on social media, then scroll through others achieving their (much bigger) goals. We find value in our work, until we retire or get made redundant. We take pride in how we're raising a family, until our kids embarrass us, or leave, or the relationship breaks down. A friend recently said to me, 'I don't do anything that important. I'm just a mum, and I'm not very good at that either.'

We sometimes find it hard to see our value.

My friend Simon used to be an auctioneer. One day, his company received a pair of vases. I find it hard to get excited about vases, but I'm assured these were really nice ones. So nice, in fact, that the auctioneers valued them at around

£800 to £1,000 for the set. Not bad for some fancy flowerpots ...

What they'd failed to notice was that these vases were made from imperial Chinese porcelain. When they were advertised for sale, the original owner tracked them down and made an offer in order to redeem what previously belonged to them.

The final sum?

£45,000.

Simon will tell you, the true value of any item is what someone is willing to pay. And in the case of the Chinese vases, the one to whom they belonged was willing to pay a high price to bring them home.

As we've seen in the previous chapter, Jesus' death was the price-tag on our freedom. But what does that say about our value, our worth to him?

If you'd been on the execution hill that day, witnessing the blood-soaked agony of Jesus on the cross, you'd have been surrounded by noise. Deep cries of grief from some, but a lot more was coming from the mocking of the crowd:

'All hail the king!' as they spat at him.

'Save yourself, if you really are the Son of God!' while pointing fingers.

'He saved others, but he can't save himself!' between the laughs.

They mocked because they thought Jesus was just another random local good guy, who got caught up in his own hype, then ended up with the death sentence for claiming to be the Son of God. But the irony is that their insults were so accurate. Jesus really was the 'king' of heaven come to rescue his people. He really was 'saving others' by dying for them in that moment.

The noise dies down after Jesus' final breath leaves his body. But, standing there, you'd have heard one more voice. A Roman centurion who'd watched Jesus die gets it right. 'This man truly was the Son of God!'[6]

The Bible says that the Son of God is eternally and infinitely precious: 'For you know that God paid a ransom to save you,' says Peter, one of Jesus' disciples. 'And it was not paid with mere gold or silver … It was [paid with] the precious

---

6   Mark 15:39

blood of Christ ...'[7] In other words, God didn't pay for our salvation in cash at auction. He paid with the most perfect and precious life imaginable.

If you'd been stood on that execution hill, you wouldn't have merely been watching the death of a random local good guy. You'd have seen the infinitely precious Son of God dying for you.

You may be winning at life, and love answering the question 'what do you do?' because it gives you a chance to tell the rest of us how well it's going. You may have been through experiences that have made you feel damaged or devalued. Worthless. Insignificant.

But however significant or insignificant you feel, the one to whom you belong was willing to pay the ultimate and infinite price to bring you home, your eternal home in heaven.

You – in your small corner of the world, reading this little book – are significant to the God who created the entire cosmos. He loves *you*.

When we follow Jesus, our fundamental value is found in the cost of Good Friday. We

---

7   1 Peter 1:18–19

can stop looking to our possessions, positions and property to give us a sense of significance. Instead, our value and worth becomes found in him. When we belong to him, it prevents the pride or perils of answering the question 'what do you do?'.

You are more significant to God than you could ever have imagined.

PEACE

I'm a lover, not a fighter.

Seriously. My friends have tried to get me involved in their mixed martial arts classes. I call it Fight Club to their faces (and Wrestling Parties behind their backs). There's no way. I don't want to hurt anyone (although let's be honest, it's much more likely to be me getting hurt). I don't want to fight anyone. I don't want to be anyone's enemy.

Whether martial arts is your thing or not, we see people fighting everywhere, making enemies of each other. We open our news apps and the world is at war. Political parties tear each other down. Neighbours fall out and there's awkwardness on the street. We're hurt by someone we care about and the relationship is stained. We long for peace. But it seems pretty rare.

Why is that? Why do we struggle to find peace with those around us? And come to think of it, why do we struggle to find peace within ourselves?

The Roman Empire attempted to bring peace by crushing all opposition, and any hint of rebellion led to brutal consequences. Jesus wasn't the only one who'd been executed that day. Two convicts had hung next to him on their own crosses. An ugly sign to the world not to step out of line. But resentment boiled under the surface.

One of the criminals had hurled insults at Jesus, defiant until his final breath. He'd raged in agony, and Jesus had borne the brunt of his anger. Some of us can be a bit like that. We're angry with God. We're angry at the hand we've been dealt and the world around us. Inside, resentment boils.

Others of us aren't as vocal, but we still feel the strain of tension with others, we're trying to keep the peace but lack the harmony we'd love to possess.

The Bible diagnoses the problem. Like a doctor bearing bad news, it's hard to hear, but we must hear it to get the cure. The Bible holds up the truth like a mirror showing us what we're really like. And it shows us the root cause of our lack of peace in life …

We are not at peace with God.

Instinctively we push God away and want to call the shots in our own lives. We might not show it like the criminal who'd hurled insults at Jesus, but there remains a massive barrier of sin between us and God. In fact, our sin makes us God's enemies. And our sin spills over into all our other relationships too. It ruins the peace in our relationship with God, with other people, and even ourselves.

But it doesn't have to be that way. While one criminal had raged against Jesus, the other criminal had seen things differently. 'We deserve to die for our crimes,' he'd said, 'but this man [Jesus] hasn't done anything wrong.'

He'd seen the problem wasn't everyone else, but admitted his own sin. Rather than push Jesus away, he'd pushed for reconciliation. And he found it.

He asked: 'Jesus, remember me when you come into your Kingdom.' And Jesus had answered him, 'I assure you, today you will be with me in paradise.'[8]

What's going on here?

If you were to ask me what makes someone a Christian – indeed, if you were to ask me what gets someone to heaven – I'd point you to that convict. It doesn't mean living a good life. It doesn't mean having everything figured out. That man had no opportunity to earn forgiveness by doing good stuff.

Instead he recognised he'd done wrong and he was on the 'enemy' side of God. But he'd also realised that Jesus, rather than crushing his enemies like the Roman Empire, was there dying for them. He'd asked for forgiveness, and through that, and that alone, the criminal had been reconciled to God. In that moment, he went from an enemy to a friend.

That's the good news of Good Friday.

We can have peace with God in exactly the same way. We recognise we've done wrong. We

---

8   Luke 23:39–43

request forgiveness. We reconcile with God. That's it.

And when we've got peace with God, that changes us. We find the power to forgive others when we realise how much we have been forgiven by God. It's a great leveller. It's much harder for me to hold something against my neighbour when I know God himself holds nothing against me.

The same is true of inner peace. If you're anything like me, we keep a mental list of mistakes we've made in life, which we find hard to let go of – a record of wrongs and regrets that we keep bringing back up in our minds.

When we ask God for his forgiveness, he promises never to bring it up with us again. God doesn't remind you of your past, or hold it against you. And if he isn't going to bring it up with us, then we don't have to either.

That makes my soul breathe a sigh of relief. You too?

True peace is truly three-dimensional – vertical with God, horizontal with others, inner with yourself. You can find it. It begins with finding peace with God. It begins with Jesus' death that first Easter weekend.

MEANING

'This is where the rubber hits the road, isn't it?'

Chris looked his dad in the eye, searching for some reassurance.

The paramedics were about to move Chris and his wife Anna's newborn son Samuel to another hospital via ambulance, and things weren't looking good.

Chris had been brought up in a Christian family, his dad the leader of a local church. He'd heard all about things like 'hope' and 'trust' in God during hard times, but had never had much need to put theory into practice, until now.

Samuel had been born with a heart defect that hadn't been picked up during any of the pregnancy scans, and he wasn't responding well to treatment. A sickening cocktail of fear and confusion was swirling around in the minds of the whole family.

Including mine.

My nephew Sam was with us for three days.

It's the smallness of the coffin that sticks with you. I couldn't tell you what the weather was like on the day of the funeral because in the cemetery everything seemed grey. Take that cocktail from a few days before, and add to it large measures of devastation, disappointment, distress and despair.

If you were to take a screenshot of that moment, it would look very much like the Saturday of the first Easter weekend. Jesus' disciples had huge hopes. There was so much expectation placed on Jesus and what he would go on to do, not to mention the fact that he was a loved brother, son and friend. And now he was gone. They'd watched his final breaths leave his butchered body.

Why had God let this happen? Why was God allowing people to experience the full depths of darkest despair? Where was God in this pain and suffering?

It would be understandable for Jesus' first followers to have been asking these questions.

34

It was understandable for Chris and Anna, too. And it is understandable for you, in the middle of your own personal pain and suffering.

Is there any *meaning* to this moment?

Is there any *meaning* to anything? Depression, diagnosis, disease, death, disappointment …

Of course, atheism would have to answer 'nope'. 'Life is meaningless,' said Tim Minchin in his speech at the University of Western Australia. 'I think it's absurd: the idea of seeking meaning in the set of circumstances that happens to exist after 13.8 billion years' worth of unguided events. Leave it to humans to think the universe has a purpose for them.'[9]

If you believe we came from nothing, and we're headed towards nothing in the end, then this short bit in the middle – this brief time lived as insignificant specks of dust on a rock hurtling around one of many, many stars – seems pretty pointless. Why *shouldn't* the randomness of the universe deal you some cold, confusing cards?

But we don't live like that, do we? None of us would look Chris and Anna in the eye, shrug our shoulders, and say 'Well, what did you expect?!'

---

9   Tim Minchin, *9 Life Lessons – Tim Minchin UWA Address*, YouTube, 8 Oct 2013

I hope no one has said that to you in the middle of your pain and suffering either.

We yearn for meaning.

We're all living in the Saturday.

For Jesus' friends, there was no expectation that things would turn out okay in the end. They were in the cold pit of confusion. But even though they couldn't see it or sense it, God was still in control of the situation. There was a plan and a purpose. There was meaning to the moment. God let the disciples experience the full extent of the confusion and pain of Saturday because something glorious would rise from it.

Easter Saturday reminds us that nothing happens outside of his care and control. He knows how you're feeling. He knows and relates to the full extent of the human experience, including our worst pain. He weaves purpose into our situation and even, if we're trusting in him, can use it for our own good. It should never be used as a simple or shallow answer to anything, but the Bible claims that somehow 'in all things God works for the good of those who love him'[10] even if we can't see it or sense it.

---

10 Romans 8:28, NIV

All things?

Even the death of Jesus?
Even Samuel's story?
Even the things you've been through?

All things for 'those who love him'.

Entering into that loving relationship with God through Jesus won't mean all suffering suddenly makes sense, or goes away. In fact, Jesus warns us that life can become harder when we become Christians. We will meet opposition and hostility because of our faith. But in the pit of pain there's a promise – that nothing is outside of God's care and control.

It's impossible to tell exactly what good can come of Samuel's story. But Chris and Anna will tell you that his life was not without meaning, nor was the pain and suffering they went through. At the thanksgiving service that followed Samuel's burial, they spoke of trust in God, and the real hope of heaven because of what happened on that first Easter.

We're all living in the Saturday.
But Sunday is coming.

HAPPINESS

'Excuse me, do you have a few moments to complete a quick survey? Wonderful!'

1. How happy did you feel yesterday?
2. Do you feel the things you do in your life are worthwhile?
3. Overall, how satisfied are you with your life?

These are some of the questions the Office for National Statistics ask to determine well-being in the UK. And one thing is clear from the recent results: happiness is on the decline.

Despite living in the height of expressive individualism, scores for happiness and life satisfaction are lower than ever across all demographics (although if you're interested in the stats, women are less happy than men, and the least happy decade to be in is your fifties). The survey also shows that how happy we are can depend on very changeable things like our age, our physical health, our relationship status and our employment situations.[11]

If you're anything like me, your levels of happiness can yo-yo up and down. They can be affected on a day-by-day, even hour-by-hour, basis by all kinds of things. A chocolate bar. A rain cloud. Someone's opinion of us. How well things are going at home or at work. External circumstances affect our internal happiness all the time. Happiness fluctuates.

But the events of Easter allow us not merely to experience shallow, temporary, fluctuating happiness, but deep, lasting *joy*.

That was Mary's experience …

There are quite a few Marys in the Bible. Jesus' mother Mary stood at the cross on Good Friday. Watching her son suffer felt like a sword piercing her soul. Another Mary wept alongside her. This other Mary got up early on Sunday morning and went to Jesus' tomb. As if the sadness of Saturday

---

11 *Personal Well-being in the UK: April 2022 to March 2023*, Office for National Statistics UK, 7 Nov 2023

wasn't bad enough, her despair deepened as she found the tomb empty. Had the body been stolen?

The Bible says she stood outside in tears. Perhaps you've been there.

Over the sound of her sobs, she hears the gentle voice of a man behind her. 'Why are you crying?' he asks. 'Who are you looking for?' Desperate for answers, Mary pleads with the man 'Tell me where you have put him!'

'Mary …'

She turns to look.

It's Jesus.

It's really him! They'd loved him and followed him. They'd watched him die and buried him. And now here he was, living and breathing and talking and smiling and meeting her in the middle of her pain.

And in that moment, everything changed.

Her cries of despair turn to cries of joy. 'I have seen the Lord!'[12]

Maybe Mary should have expected it? Before Jesus died, he'd told his friends: 'I will see you again; then you will rejoice, and no one can rob you of that joy.'[13] They didn't get it at the time but afterwards it all became clear.

12 John 20:11–18

13 John 16:22

It changed everything! When Jesus rose from the dead it proved that everything he'd taught could be trusted. It announced he really was and is the Son of God. It showed he can deliver on his promises. The love and freedom and peace and significance and hope we crave is offered by the man who beat death and walked out of the grave on Easter Sunday morning. It meant that eternal life was on offer.

And those things aren't changeable. They aren't affected by your external circumstances.

Mary wasn't just a bit *happier*. She was experiencing true *joy*. No doubt Mary's happiness levels fluctuated throughout the rest of her life despite meeting the risen Jesus. But from that moment on, her joy underpinned her changing emotions. If happiness is up and down like the crashing waves, then joy is like the depths of the ocean underneath them.

Her true joy came from knowing personally the one who gives a life of contentment and satisfaction, which goes on forever, to anyone who asks him.

That was Mary's experience because of Easter Sunday. It can be yours too.

OPTIMISM

None of us were sure whether Iris would make it through the summer.

Being admitted to hospital at 90 years old is never a good thing, but especially when the doctors say you've got kidney failure. I remember sitting by her bed with her husband Malcolm, in the overly-warm hospital ward. Malcolm was bright and cheerful, full of encouragement and smiles as usual, despite his dear wife's prognosis.

As I left the ward, I remember promising Iris that I would bring her back a shell from my holiday, thinking to myself 'I really hope you're still here for me to give it to you when I get back.'

Amazingly, Iris rallied, and after a few weeks she was home.

But that Christmas, Malcolm collapsed. By Boxing Day he was gone.

'I wouldn't want him back!' Iris said, catching me a little off-guard. I was stood with her in the bright winter sunshine outside the crematorium. We'd just had Malcolm's funeral, and Iris was smiling. But it wasn't a fake smile. It wasn't painted on for appearances. She was experiencing something more than just surface-level smiles.

'I wouldn't want him back, because I know where he is now, and it's better by far.'

She was experiencing *hope*.

Hope beats optimism. I'm sure you know some glass-half-full people. For these unicorns, life is one big rainbow – unlike the Eeyores among us, for whom it's one big rain cloud. But even for those who usually see the bright side of life, things don't always get better. Sometimes there's no silver lining, no sunshine after the rain.

When the journey of life is rough, we can sometimes slap on a smile, sellotape a toilet roll tube to our foreheads and try really hard to be a unicorn. But fundamentally we need a sense of hope that goes beyond the sunny disposition of mere optimism.

Even if you have much to be pessimistic about, you can still live with hope.

Where did Iris get hope from?

She got it from Easter Sunday.

After Mary finds the tomb empty, and finds herself in conversation with the resurrected Jesus, she rushes to tell the others. By that same evening, Jesus had met with more and more people – eyewitnesses everywhere. They talk, walk, eat, laugh and pray together – on another occasion they even have a BBQ on the beach![14] Jesus was there in the touchable flesh.

He had defeated death.

On the Friday, Jesus had gone into the depths of death, and by Sunday morning he'd burst through the other side. Imagine a train going through the darkest of tunnels or a needle going through the blackest of fabrics. When we put our life – and death – in his hands, the Bible says 'now we also may live new lives. Since we have been united with him … we will also be raised to life as he was.'[15] Joined to Jesus, we are like the carriages pulled through by the train; the thread pulled through by the needle.

---

14 I'm not joking! Check out John 21:1–14

15 Romans 6:4–5

That means death is now no longer the final word for anyone who believes and trusts in him.

That can include you.

When we connect with Jesus, eternal life is ours. Heaven is our home, our final destination.

Leaving Iris' hospital ward that summer to go on holiday, we got in the car and drove eight hours to Cornwall. It felt like eight days. The traffic was terrible. The car was boiling. The kids were loud. The roads were bumpy. But we knew Cornwall was the destination, and Cornwall is fantastic. That made the journey bearable. Without the knowledge of the destination, the journey would have been pointless and painful. The destination makes a difference to the journey, right?

Our ultimate destination really matters. It makes a difference to the journey of life. So what's yours? Is there *nothing* after we die, no point, no reality? Could it be worse – if there's a heaven, could there be a hell? Because Jesus taught there's both, and his resurrection shows he knows what he's talking about. If there's no hope of heaven, then what are you ultimately optimistic about?

When life gets tough we need much more than a holiday or a night out or a promotion or a sporting win to get us through. All of us – Iris, Malcolm, me, you – need much more on the horizon. When we know our final destination is heaven, it makes even the roughest journey in life bearable, rather than just pointless and painful. The hope of heaven goes beyond just looking forward to the next good experience in our short few decades of life.

I'd never been to a funeral filled with such hope and joy until I'd been to Malcolm's. I'd like mine to be like that.

Would you?

Like Malcolm, put your life in Jesus' hands, and death won't be the final word for you either.

SECURITY

Your password has to include seventeen characters, two and a half capital letters, nine odd numbers and a special character (but only from their choice of special characters!). Oh, and you have to stand on one leg while typing it. Passwords are so hard to remember these days, you can get apps that remember them for you. The one design flaw? You need a password to get into the app!

We're obsessed with security. But while carefully creating passwords is something we *can* do, it feels like so many factors for personal security in life are very much out of our hands.

Take for example our finances. As long as you're in credit everything will be okay, but the thought of opening your banking app one morning and seeing the whole thing drained has serious implications.

Or how about your job security. The long-term trajectory of your career might be an exciting prospect, but finding out there's been a takeover and you're at risk of redundancy would be a world-shaker.

It may be that our safe place is our home. A lock on the door and the calm within our four walls can give us a sense of protection, but as crime rates rise, or a house stops being home for whatever reason, we start scrolling for somewhere new to live.

It may be the various relationships we have, from parents to partners. We need emotional security from them, but if something happens to the relationship – or to them – we feel like the rug has been pulled from under our feet.

Hear me right: none of those things are *bad* things! It's okay to have money in the bank, apply for that job, and be in a relationship. But the very things that give us a sense of security don't seem to be particularly, well, secure. Ultimately they can't guarantee the absolute stability, complete reliability, real safety, and unshakable security we need.

But Easter can.

Jesus said to his friends: 'Don't let your hearts be troubled.'[16] What, even when the bank balance is low? Even when work dries up or the diagnosis comes? Even when our friendships and relationships and prospects dissolve?

When trouble hits, we crave a sense of reassurance. Research into human psychology tells us we need a strong sense of 'home' in order to feel safe – 'a place of refuge, comfort and security' in the words of an article in *Psychology Today*.[17] So what's Jesus' plan?

Jesus goes on: 'There is more than enough room in my Father's home [heaven]. If this were not so, would I have told you that I am going to prepare a place for you?' Jesus is offering the ultimate home, the ultimate place of refuge, comfort and security. Jesus' death and resurrection secures you a place in heaven if you'll accept it – a place where you're ultimately safe forever, no matter what happens to you now.

'When everything is ready,' Jesus adds, 'I will come and get you, so that you will always be

---

16 John 14:1

17 Diane E. Dreher, *Where Do You Feel at Home?*, Psychology Today, 3 Feb 2024

with me where I am. And you know the way to where I am going.'

One of Jesus' friends, Thomas, needed to know for sure. He asked: 'how can we know the way?' Jesus answered with the calm clarity that our insecure hearts need: *'I am* the way'.[18]

This is going to sound corny, so bear with me. But it's important to remember it, so here goes ...

The password is Jesus.

He is *the* special character.

Heaven can be your home only through him. There's no other way of accessing eternal security, other than through the one whose death and resurrection secures it for you.

You know the way to that place. It's Jesus himself. Easter has made sure of it.

---

18 John 14:2–6

WHAT'S YOUR STORY?

My friend David looked out of his window into the garden. He watched as one of those massive pigeons landed on a tree branch. It sat there for a few seconds, but this particular branch was far too weak to hold our feathered friend. As the branch slowly gave way under the weight of the pigeon, the bird urgently flew off to find a stronger place to rest.

The things and people in our lives are like that branch. They're not strong enough to bear the full weight of our expectations. When we put the 'heaviness' of our need for real love, significance, security, peace, hope and joy onto things or other people, they inevitably bend and break. We fly off asking again 'what's next?'.

So what's your story? Where are you looking for all the things you've ever wanted? On who or what are you putting the heavy weight of those expectations?

They're all fantastic things, I'm sure! But they're not ultimate things.

They're good. But they're not God.

They're gifts. But they're not the Giver.

Could it be that when we're searching in all those places for love, significance, freedom, peace, meaning, security, joy and hope, it's actually God himself we're searching for? Like thirst and hunger show us our need for water and food, what if our lack of contentment in life shows us our need for him? What if all these good gifts are pointing us towards our need for the good Giver? What if all our relationships are pointing us towards our need for a relationship with God? I don't just need what he can give me, I need *him*.

When we realise that only a relationship with God can give us everything we've ever wanted, it means we can enjoy those gifts even more …

I can enjoy my relationships more, knowing they're not the ultimate source of love in my life. I can enjoy my job more, knowing it's not my ultimate source of meaning or significance or purpose. I can enjoy the things I own more, knowing they're not my ultimate source of security or happiness. I can enjoy my life experiences more, knowing they're not my ultimate source of hope or joy.

This can be your story. Jesus' death and resurrection means that you and I can have a relationship with God forever. Easter shows that you have been fully loved by him. You are significant to him. You can belong to him and have proper security in him. Heaven doesn't just make us vaguely optimistic, but gives us firm, trustworthy hope in a coming reality, a final destination that makes sense of the journey. And heaven is for those who believe and trust in Jesus – the Jesus who one stunning weekend made a way for anyone, including you, to have all you truly want and need: a relationship with God.

The invitation is to enter into that relationship. You can do that on the next page, if you want to.

WHAT'S NEXT?

PRAY

'Father God, I'm not exactly sure of all the details – I've still got questions and lots to think about. But if it's true that you can give me real and lasting love, significance, peace, freedom, security, meaning, hope and joy, then that's what I want. It's what I've always wanted. I'm sorry for looking everywhere else for it apart from you. I'm sorry for the sin in the dark corners of my life. Thank you for Jesus, for his death and resurrection on that first Easter, which makes relationship with you possible in the first place. Please come into my life and help me by your Spirit to figure out what a new relationship with you looks like now, until I'm secure with you in heaven forever. Amen.'

ASK

This book may have raised more questions than it's answered. That's very normal and very good! Maybe someone handed you this book, talk to them about it. I am certain they'd be so happy for you to ask them about their experience of being a Christian and how it's changed their life. And if they can't answer all your questions, I'll bet they can find someone who can.

WATCH

Some of those questions may get answered in a superb series of short videos called '321', looking at who Jesus is and how to see life with him. Scan the QR code to get started.

VISIT

Church isn't just for Christians. Every Sunday different people from different backgrounds just turn up at church to find out for themselves what all the fuss is about. Maybe this is a good time for you to join them. Ask any Christians you know if you can visit their church with them (they'll definitely say yes!).

READ

For more about the historical evidence behind the events of Easter, see *The Case For Easter: A Journalist Investigates Evidence for the Resurrection* by Lee Strobel.

Or to think more about the meaning of Easter, see *Heaven, How I Got Here: The Story of the Thief on the Cross* by Colin S. Smith.

For more on Jesus direct from the Bible, see the Gospel written by John.

More books from 10Publishing

Resources that point to Jesus